Contents

Forces and Motion

What are forces and motion?

Forces are pushes and pulls that act on objects. They make things move, stop, get squeezed or change shape or direction. For example, when you throw a ball, muscles in your arm pull on your bones, making your arm move. Your moving arm pushes the ball, making it fly through the air. As it goes, the force of air resistance slows it down, and the force of gravity eventually pulls it to the ground.

Forces are happening everywhere, all around us, all the time. They play a part whenever we move or make anything else move. They keep planes up in the air and send rockets to the Moon. They control the way a river flows to the sea, and the way the planets orbit around the Sun. Forces inside your body make all your body parts and cells work.

Forces can be visible or invisible, close-up or far away, strong or weak. They can be divided into many different types, such as pressure, friction, gravity and magnetism.

Staying still

Even when an object isn't moving, forces are acting on it. For example, an egg stays on a table because gravity is pulling it towards the Earth. But the table pushes it up against the force of gravity. The forces are in balance, so they cancel each other out and the egg stays still.

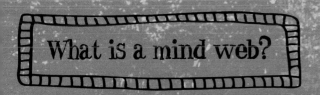

What is a mind web?

This book uses mind webs to show all the facts about forces in a quick, easy-to-understand way. A mind web lays out all the information about a topic – such as gravity – on one page. The topic name goes in the middle, and words and facts about the topic are arranged around it, with lines linking them together. The mind webs in this book also have little pictures to help you remember things.

Mind webs are helpful for revising and learning the basics of a subject. It can also be useful to draw your own mind web when you want to brainstorm an idea or make quick notes about what you know. Mind webs are also sometimes known as spider charts, spidergrams or mind maps. The mini mind web below shows the areas of the topic 'Forces and motion'.

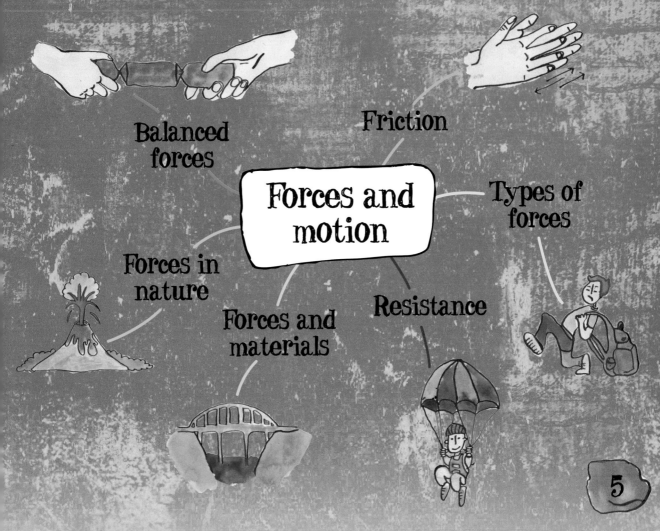

Balanced forces

Friction

Forces and motion

Types of forces

Forces in nature

Resistance

Forces and materials

Types of forces

While all forces push or pull, they can work in different ways and there are many different types. If two objects have to be touching for a force to work, it is known as a contact force. For example, a finger pressing a doorbell, your hand squeezing a ball of clay and the wind making a flag flap are all contact forces.

If a force can work across a gap, it is called a force at a distance, a distant force or an 'action-at-a-distance' force. Magnetism works at a distance in this way. A magnet can pull a metal object towards it, even if it is not touching the object. Gravity is another example of a force that can work at a distance, even across vast areas of empty space.

Measuring force
Force is measured in units called Newtons, named after the great scientist Isaac Newton. The force of gravity on a large apple measures about 1 Newton. As well as having a measurable strength, a force also always has a direction.

Moon's gravity

static electric charge

tides

magnetic fishing toy

Forces at a distance

dropped egg falling to floor

gravity

Earth's magnetism

moves compass needle

speed up

Effects of forces

move

slow down

makes objects

break

change shape

stop

squeezing clay

water pressure

grip of rubber soles

kicking a ball

Contact forces

carrying heavy bag

turning a steering wheel

Types of forces

Measuring forces

unit of measurement

Newton

pulls objects together

force needed to accelerate a 1kg weight at 1m per second per second

gravity

Examples of forces

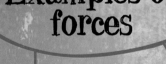

magnetism

friction

upthrust

rubbing slows objects

floats objects

pulls and pushes objects

pressure

squeezes / pushes objects

Gravity

Gravity is a force that pulls objects towards each other. The more mass an object has – meaning the more matter, or stuff, it contains – the more gravity it has.

In everyday life, we think of gravity as pulling things down. This is because we live on a very large object, the Earth. It's much bigger than any other object nearby, so its gravity pulls everything else, like cars, rocks and humans, towards it. Wherever you are on the Earth, its gravity pulls you towards its centre.

Near and far
Gravity works at a distance. But the closer together two objects are, the more powerful the force of gravity between them. That's why, if you jump off a wall close to the ground, gravity will quickly pull you down. But if you fly into space, the pull of Earth's gravity becomes weaker and weaker, so astronauts inside a space station can float around in mid-air. This low gravity is called microgravity.

have mass (amount of matter)

= pull of gravity on mass

all objects are made of matter

more gravity

Weight

more weight

less gravity

less weight

Falling objects

air resistance slows objects down

in a vacuum

all objects fall at the same speed

as an object falls, it accelerates

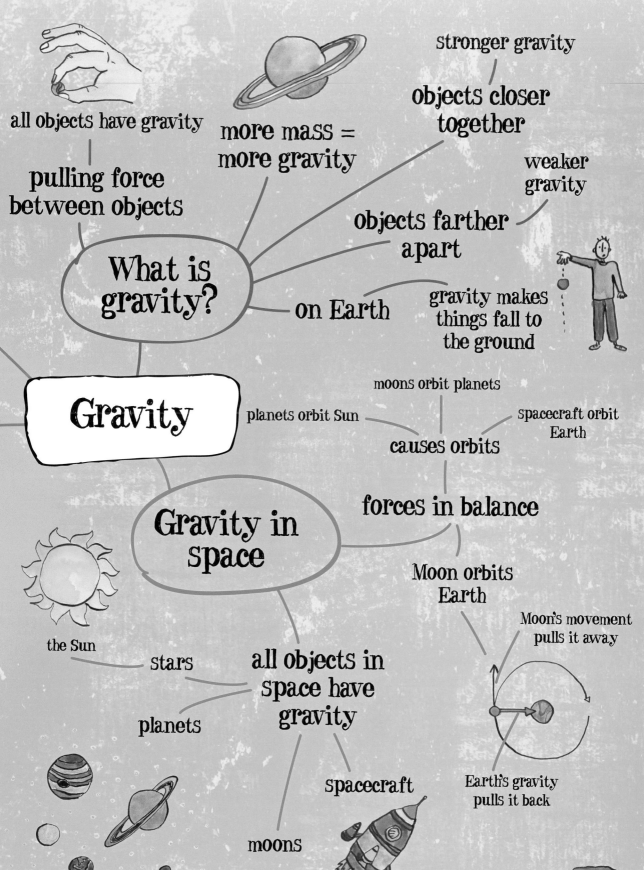

all objects have gravity

pulling force between objects

more mass = more gravity

stronger gravity

objects closer together

weaker gravity

objects farther apart

What is gravity?

on Earth

gravity makes things fall to the ground

Gravity

moons orbit planets

planets orbit Sun

spacecraft orbit Earth

causes orbits

forces in balance

Gravity in space

Moon orbits Earth

Moon's movement pulls it away

the Sun

stars

planets

all objects in space have gravity

Earth's gravity pulls it back

spacecraft

moons

9

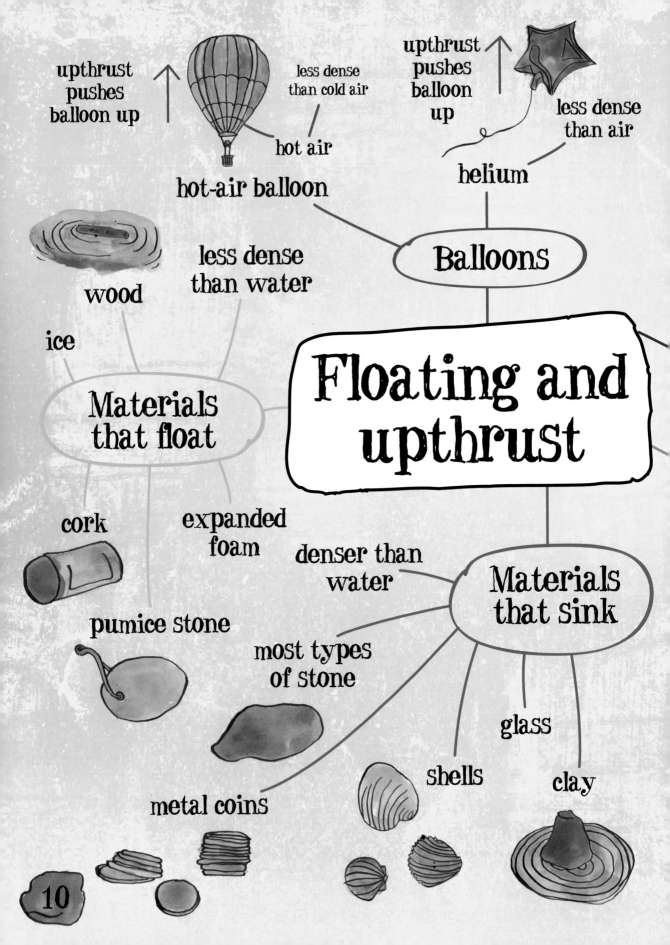

Floating and upthrust

Balloons

upthrust pushes balloon up

less dense than cold air

hot air

hot-air balloon

upthrust pushes balloon up

less dense than air

helium

Materials that float

wood

ice

less dense than water

cork

expanded foam

pumice stone

Materials that sink

denser than water

most types of stone

metal coins

shells

glass

clay

10

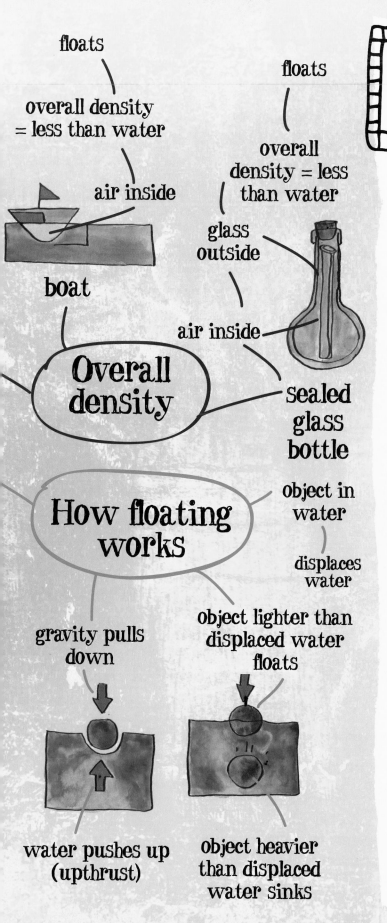

floats

overall density
= less than water

air inside

boat

floats

overall
density = less
than water

glass
outside

air inside

sealed
glass
bottle

Overall density

How floating works

object in water

displaces water

object lighter than displaced water floats

gravity pulls down

water pushes up (upthrust)

object heavier than displaced water sinks

When you put an object into water, it takes up space. To do this, it pushes some of the water out of the way, or displaces it. The rest of the water pushes up on the object, in the place where water used to be. This pushing force is called upthrust.

If the object is lighter than the water it has displaced, the force of upthrust can hold it up. But if it is heavier than the water it has displaced, the gravity pulling on it is greater than the upthrust, and it sinks.

Density
Density means how heavy an object is for its size. Objects sink if they are denser than water, and float if they are less dense than water. The density of an object can include the air inside it. This is why boat shapes can float even when they are made of metal — because the air inside them changes their density.

Objects can float in or on other substances too. For example, a hot air or helium balloon floats in the air.

Pressure

Whenever things touch, they apply pressure. This force is happening all around us all the time. Your feet on the floor, bricks stacked up to make buildings, a pencil drawing a line on paper – it's all pressure. The amount of pressure depends on the strength of the pushing force, and the area of contact. The pressure equals the force divided by the area. For example, imagine pressing onto a block of cheese with a knife edge and a flat ruler, both using the same amount of force. With the ruler, the force is spread out over a wide surface area, so the pressure is weak. But the knife edge has much less area, so the same amount of force means a lot more pressure, and it cuts through the cheese easily.

Air and water pressure
Solids, liquids and gases can all apply pressure. The deeper underwater you go, the more you are squeezed by water pressure. The air in the atmosphere also presses on us all the time, though we are used to it and don't notice it.

fire
extinguisher

Gas
pressure

Pressure

used in

hairspray
can

squirty
cream

Water
pressure

pressure of water
on objects in it

deep-sea
submersible

greater depth
= greater
pressure

strong walls
and windows

solids

pushing
force

liquids

gases

contact
between

sharp pencil

knife

less area = more
pressure

caterpillar
tracks

pressure =
force divided
by area

more area
= less pressure

What is pressure?

balloons

pushing force
of air

atmospheric
pressure

Air pressure

straw

sucking

atmospheric
pressure

drink forced up

Everyday pressure

wind

air pressure
pushes
windmill

machine
parts

blood pressure

vehicles on
roads

pressure of blood
on blood vessels

feet on
pavements

buildings

Friction

Friction is a force that slows down or stops objects when they slide, scrape or rub past each other. Rough and rubbery surfaces have more friction than smooth ones. That's why rubber-soled trainers with lots of ridges are good at gripping steep rocks, while hard, smooth skis slide easily over snow. Friction can also happen in liquids and gases. For example, there is friction between a rocket zooming through the atmosphere and the air around it. Once the rocket reaches space, however, there is no friction, as space is a vacuum with no air in it.

Friction and heat
Friction turns movement energy into heat, and makes things get warmer. That's why rubbing your hands together on a cold day warms them up.

Reducing friction
Friction can be a problem when it slows things down or wears things out. It can be reduced by coating surfaces with something slippery, like oil, known as lubrication, or by changing the shapes of objects.

14

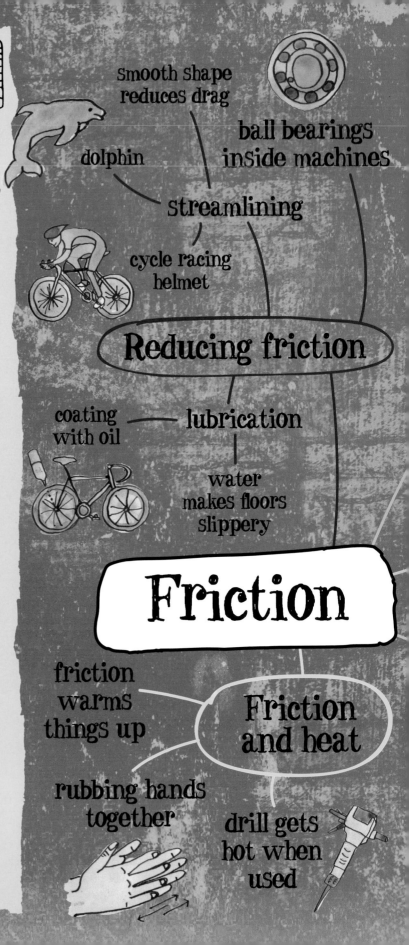

smooth shape reduces drag

dolphin

ball bearings inside machines

streamlining

cycle racing helmet

Reducing friction

coating with oil

lubrication

water makes floors slippery

Friction

friction warms things up

Friction and heat

rubbing hands together

drill gets hot when used

slows down
or stops
objects

rubbing
together

moving through
water

sliding, scraping
or rubbing force

solids

liquids

moving through air

What is friction?

gases

river wearing
away a canyon

trainers
gripping
rocks

knees
of jeans
wearing
through

Everyday friction

new shoes
rubbing feet

car skidding
on a road

Drag

friction when an
object moves through
liquid or gas

plane flying

lorry
driving

fish swimming

Balanced and unbalanced forces

Balanced forces

object is in 'equilibrium'

forces on an object cancel each other out

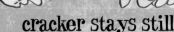

hand pulls cracker

hand pulls cracker

cracker stays still

Everyday examples

snowboarder

upthrust (up)

gravity (down)

wind (sideways)

bridge

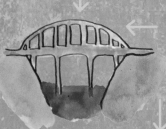

pressure from cars (down)

wind (sideways)

gravity (down)

Unbalanced forces

several forces act on an object

resultant force

forces combine to make object move

falling ball

drag

wind

gravity

ball falls to ground

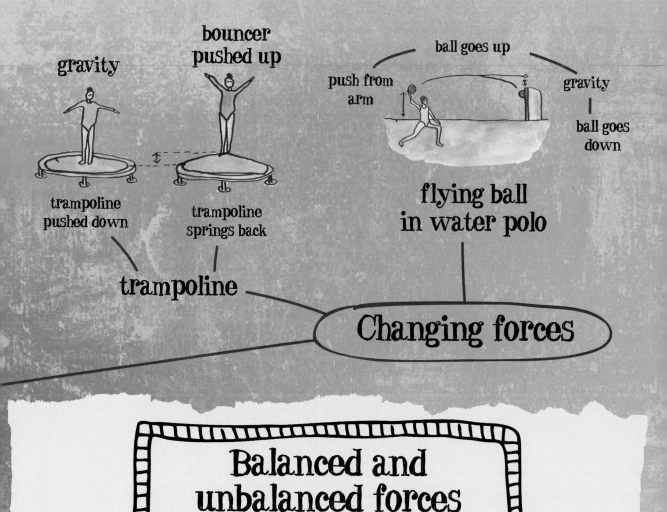

gravity

bouncer
pushed up

trampoline
pushed down

trampoline
springs back

trampoline

ball goes up

push from
arm

gravity

ball goes
down

**flying ball
in water polo**

Changing forces

Balanced and unbalanced forces

When something moves, it's because a force is pushing or pulling on it, and this force is more powerful than any other forces involved. For example, in a tug of war, two teams pull on opposite ends of a rope. If the rope moves one way, it's because one team is pulling with a stronger force.

If the rope stays still, it means the two forces pulling on the ends are in balance. Forces are still acting on the rope, but they are the same, so they cancel each other out. If something is not moving because the forces acting on it are balanced, it is said to be in equilibrium.

Resultant force
Usually, an object does not experience just one force. For example, a dropped ball falling through the air has many forces acting on it – such as pressure from the wind, drag, and gravity. The strength and direction of all these forces combine to create the force that decides what happens. This is called the resultant force.

Movement

Forces make things move. Like forces, movement is happening all around us, all the time, and is an essential part of how everything works. The movement of air and water in the atmosphere gives us our weather. Humans have to move in order to eat, speak, learn and work, and there are millions of moving parts inside us too. Machines, vehicles, animals, plants, rivers and oceans – they all move!

The way things move is also known as motion. The motion of an object can carry on unchanged, or it can change if forces act on it.

Speed and velocity
Speed means how fast an object is moving. It is measured by comparing distance moved to the time taken.

Velocity is similar to speed, but it also measures the direction an object is going in. Objects can also speed up, known as acceleration, and slow down, known as deceleration.

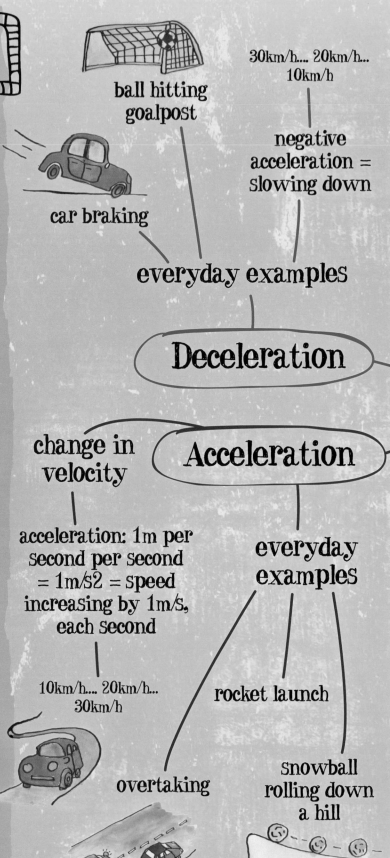

ball hitting goalpost

car braking

30km/h.... 20km/h... 10km/h

negative acceleration = slowing down

everyday examples

Deceleration

change in velocity

Acceleration

acceleration: 1m per second per second = 1m/s2 = speed increasing by 1m/s, each second

10km/h.... 20km/h... 30km/h

everyday examples

rocket launch

overtaking

snowball rolling down a hill

how things move

hand pushes

frisbee flies

forces make objects move

hand pushes

frisbee stops

Motion

forces can change an object's movement

Movement

how fast an object is moving

Speed

velocity = speed in a particular direction

acceleration: 0 = constant speed

distance divided by time

km/h = kilometres per hour — 40km/h

m/s = metres per second — 10m/s

mph = miles per hour — 500mph

Dynamics

Dynamics is the science of how forces affect movement. The father of dynamics was British scientist Isaac Newton, who lived in the 1600s and 1700s. He described how gravity works, studied light, and wrote three famous laws of motion.

Inertia and momentum
Inertia is the way objects resist change. If an object is moving, it tries to keep moving in the same way and in the same direction, unless a force acts on it to change this. If it is stationary (still), it tries to stay still until a force makes it move.

Momentum is a measurement of the way an object continues to move. It is the velocity of the object multiplied by its mass (the amount of matter in it). So, for example, a giant snowball rolling down a hill at high speed has a lot of momentum. A small one rolling downhill slowly only has a little momentum. When one object hits another, the total momentum stays the same. This is known as the conservation of momentum.

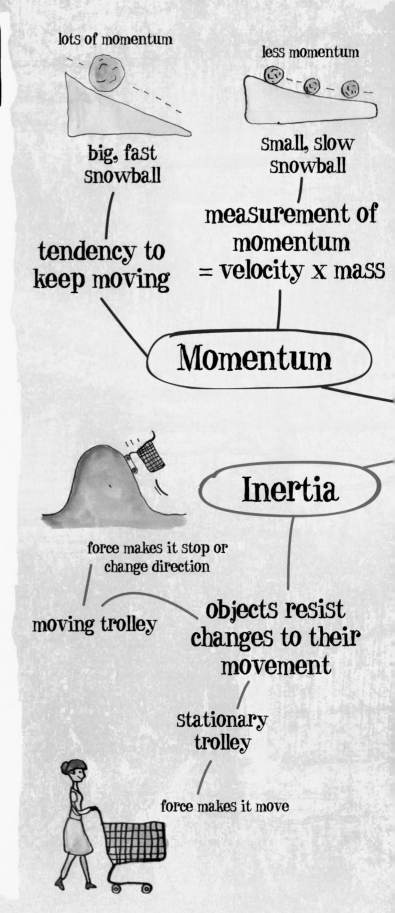

lots of momentum

less momentum

big, fast snowball

small, slow snowball

tendency to keep moving

measurement of momentum = velocity x mass

Momentum

Inertia

force makes it stop or change direction

objects resist changes to their movement

moving trolley

stationary trolley

force makes it move

pool cue hits a
pool ball

gravity holds Earth
and Moon together

how forces affect
movement

everyday
examples

dog lead stops
dog running
away

What is dynamics?

father of
dynamics

Isaac Newton
(1642–1727)

Dynamics

Moon keeps
orbiting Earth

Newton's Laws of Motion

1) objects stay
as they are
until a force
acts on them

apple on table
stays still

3) When a force
acts on an object,
the object exerts an
equal force back

2) a force acting
on an object
changes its
motion

hand picks
up apple

apple pushes
down on table

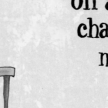

table pushes
up on apple

yoyo wants to keep moving
in a straight line

string
= centripetal force
= resistance

force pulling
towards centre
of a circle

yoyo moves
in a circle

planet orbits
Sun

Sun's gravity
= centripetal force
= resistance

planet wants to keep
moving in a straight
line

Centripetal force

slows down fall

parachute

Resistance

Useful resistance

object accelerates

Terminal velocity

brakes

gravity

slows movement
of wheels

liquid or gas

maximum
falling velocity

object falling
in a fluid

object slows down

resistance

terminal velocity

for a skydiver : approx.
200km/h (125mph)

force that resists another force

pushing force

engines

air resistance

rocket

resistance force

pulling force

gravity

What is resistance?

slide

friction

resistance force

Everyday examples

ice skating

leaf falling

climbing

resistance = friction

resistance = gravity

resistance = air resistance

When a force acts on something, it may have to overcome another force acting in the opposite direction. This is called the resistance force. For example, the pushing force of a plane's engines has to overcome the drag caused by friction with the air – also called air resistance. Resistance isn't always a problem – it can be useful. For example, opening a parachute increases air resistance to slow down a fall.

Terminal velocity
Terminal velocity is the top speed that a falling object can reach as it falls through air or water. As the object falls, pulled by gravity, it speeds up or accelerates. But the force of air or water resistance slows it down. Finally, when the two forces are in balance, the object stops accelerating, and reaches a maximum constant speed.

Centripetal force
Centripetal force is a force that pulls towards the centre of a circle. A moving object will try to keep moving in a straight line, but if it is resisted by centripetal force, this will make it move in a circle instead.

Machines

We're surrounded by machines that do all kinds of jobs for us – washing machines and dishwashers, cars, bikes, cranes and diggers. A machine is something that makes work easier by changing the way forces act on things. Even basic tools, like scissors, screwdrivers, tweezers and weighing scales, are simple machines – and most other machines are made up of similar simple parts.

Load and effort

When you have to do a job, like lifting a rock, the force you have to put in is called the effort. The force you have to overcome, such as gravity pulling on the rock, is called the load. Simple machines let you put in less effort to get the same result.

For example, lifting a large rock by hand is very hard. But if you use a lever, such as a plank resting on a brick, it's easier. You push down on the longer end of the plank, and the shorter end lifts up the rock easily.

24

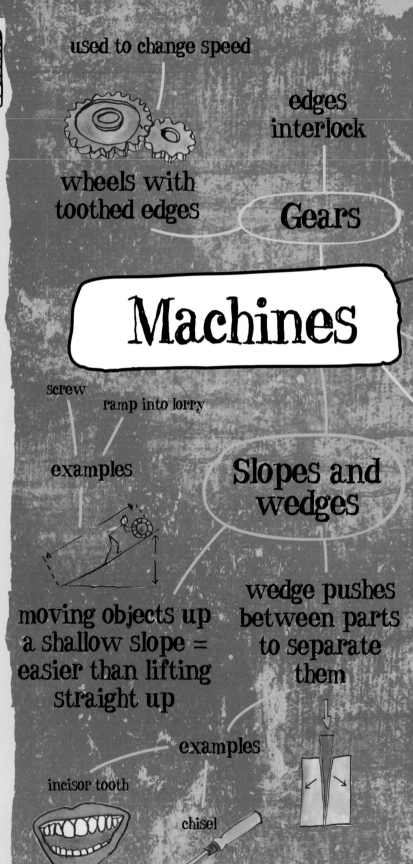

used to change speed

edges interlock

wheels with toothed edges

Gears

Machines

screw

ramp into lorry

examples

Slopes and wedges

moving objects up a shallow slope = easier than lifting straight up

wedge pushes between parts to separate them

examples

incisor tooth

chisel

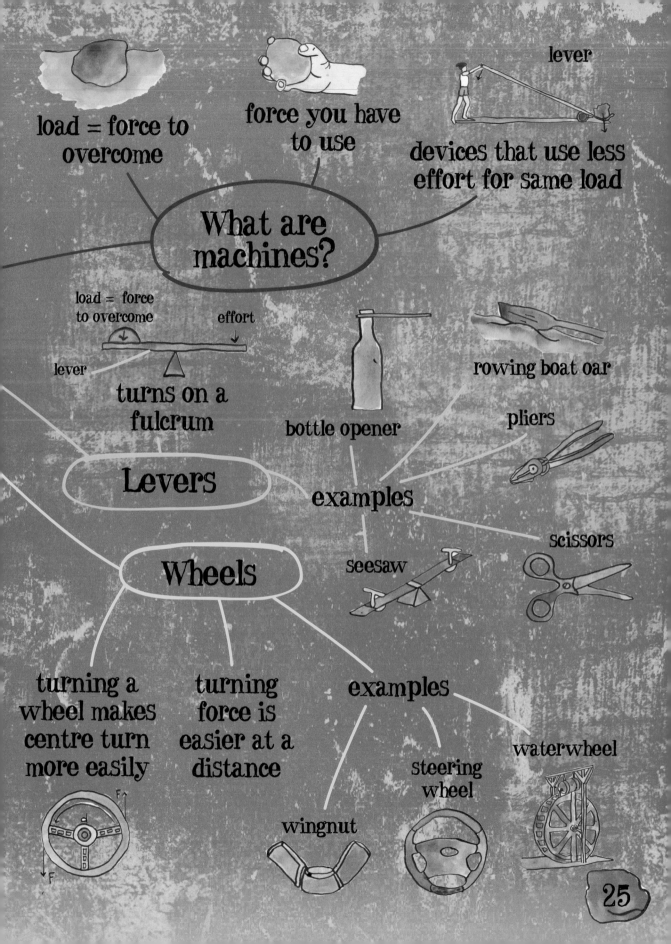

load = force to overcome

force you have to use

lever

devices that use less effort for same load

What are machines?

load = force to overcome

effort

lever

turns on a fulcrum

Levers

bottle opener

rowing boat oar

pliers

examples

scissors

Wheels

seesaw

turning a wheel makes centre turn more easily

turning force is easier at a distance

examples

steering wheel

waterwheel

wingnut

25

Forces in nature

Forces are essential to machines, buildings and vehicles, and they are a major part of science. However, forces existed long before humans did. They happen all around us in nature, as well as in modern life.

The natural world

Forces inside the Earth push sections of the crust around, causing earthquakes and creating mountain ranges. Meanwhile, gravity pulls on water, rock and soil, cutting riverbeds and wearing away hilltops. Days and seasons are a result of the forces that keep our planet orbiting around the Sun. The rising and falling of the tide happens because of the gravity between the Moon and the Earth. And weather is the result of changes in air pressure in the atmosphere, and gravity.

Living things

Plants, animals and humans have all developed on Earth and adapted ways to deal with the natural forces around us. Plants can detect gravity so they know which way to grow their roots and stems. Flying animals have developed ways to work against gravity and get off the ground.

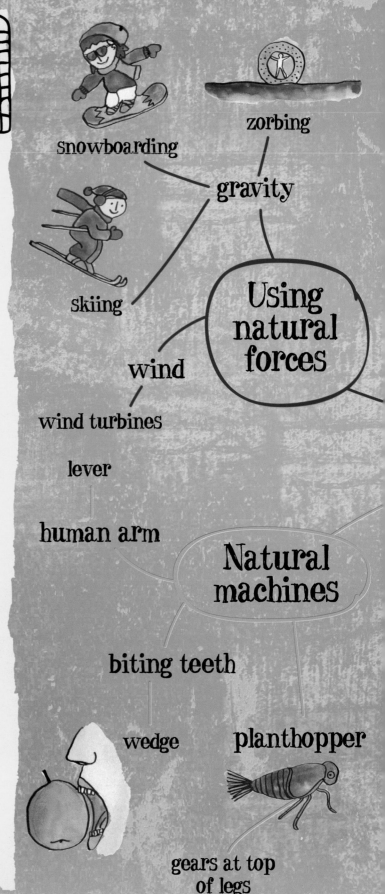

snowboarding

zorbing

gravity

skiing

Using natural forces

wind

wind turbines

lever

human arm

Natural machines

biting teeth

wedge

planthopper

gears at top of legs

cut valleys

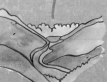
flow of rivers

erosion

glaciers

earthquakes

waves

The Earth

tides

days

volcanoes

seasons

Earth's spin

Moon's gravity

Earth's orbit

wind

Forces in nature

air pressure

Weather

gravity

pulls down rain and snow

holds atmosphere on Earth

Living with gravity

flight

birds

plants

resisting gravity

stem grows up

insects

bats

roots grow down

27

Forces and materials

Forces are happening all around us, but they can only happen because there is matter for them to act on. Matter is all the stuff that makes up objects, substances, liquids and all the other things that exist. Different types of matter are known as materials.

Forces can have different effects depending on the type of material they are acting on. For example, if you hit a glass vase with a hammer, the force will make it smash. If you hit a plank of wood just as hard with the same hammer, it might make a slight dent.

Using materials

Designers and engineers have to know how strong materials are and how they will behave when different forces act on them, in order to make sure they will work. For example, a large bridge must be strong enough to carry a lot of traffic, and withstand the forces of gravity and wind pressure without breaking. So bridges are usually made of strong, flexible materials like steel.

28

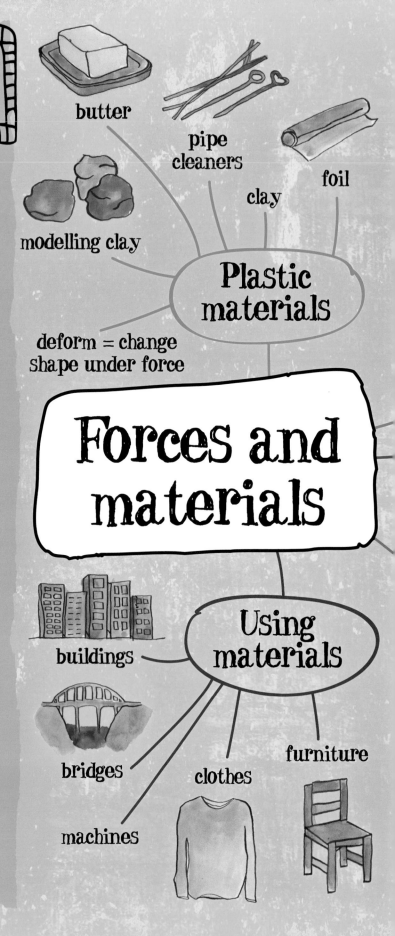

butter

pipe cleaners

foil

clay

modelling clay

Plastic materials

deform = change shape under force

Forces and materials

buildings

bridges

machines

Using materials

clothes

furniture

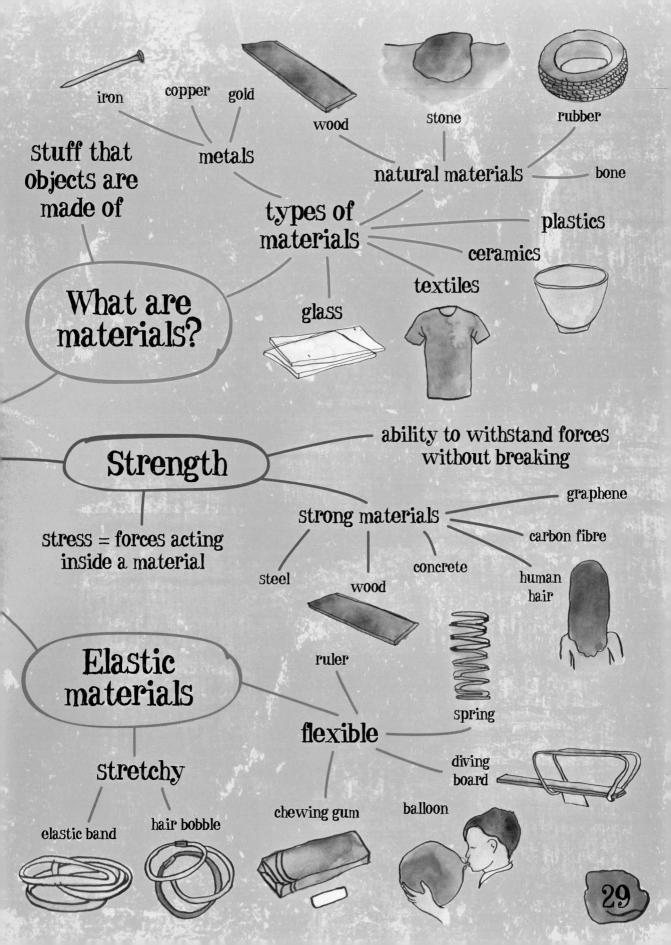

iron

copper

gold

wood

stone

rubber

bone

metals

natural materials

stuff that
objects are
made of

types of
materials

plastics

ceramics

What are
materials?

textiles

glass

Strength

ability to withstand forces
without breaking

strong materials

graphene

carbon fibre

stress = forces acting
inside a material

steel

wood

concrete

human
hair

Elastic
materials

ruler

spring

flexible

stretchy

diving
board

chewing gum

balloon

elastic band

hair bobble

29

Glossary

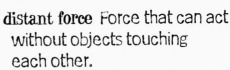

acceleration Speeding up.

adapt To change to become more suitable to the surroundings.

air resistance Force that resists the movement of an object thanks to friction with the air.

atmosphere Layer of gases surrounding a planet.

cells Tiny units that make up all living things.

centripetal force Force that pulls towards the centre of a circle.

conservation of momentum Law that says total momentum remains the same before and after objects collide.

contact force Force that can only act when one object is touching another.

deceleration Slowing down.

density How much matter a substance or object contains for its size.

displace To push something out of the way and take its place.

distant force Force that can act without objects touching each other.

drag Force that slows down an object moving in fluid, thanks to friction.

dynamics Science of how forces affect movement.

effort Force needed to make something move.

energy The power to do work or make things happen.

equilibrium State of an object when the forces acting on it are in balance.

force A push, pull or influence on an object.

force at a distance Force that can act without objects touching each other.

friction Force that slows down objects as they slide or scrape against each other.

gravity Pulling force that attracts object to each other.

inertia Tendency of objects to resist changes to their motion.

lever Stick or rod that moves at a fixed point, or fulcrum.

load Force that has to be overcome to make something move.

lubrication Reducing friction by adding a slippery substance.

magnetism An invisible force that pulls on some types of metals.

mass The amount of matter an object contains.

materials Different types of matter.

matter The stuff that objects are are made of.

microgravity Very low gravity, like that found far away from planets.

momentum Measure of an object's tendency to keep moving.

motion Another word for movement.

Newton A unit used to measure force.

orbit The path of one object in space around another.

pressure Pushing force from a solid, liquid or gas pressing on an object.

resistance Force acting against the movement of an object.

resultant force Combined effect of a number of different forces acting on an object.

speed How far an object moves in a given time.

terminal velocity Maximum velocity that an object falling through a fluid can reach.

upthrust Force of a liquid or gas pushing up on an object that is placed in it.

velocity Speed in a particular direction.

Index